The Heart Healthy Diet and Action Plan:

4 Weeks to Lower Cholesterol

and

Improved Heart Health

ALLA KAY

This book is dedicated to all the people who dislike recipes with long ingredient lists.

The Heart Healthy Diet and Action Plan:

4 Weeks to Lower Cholesterol

and

Improved Heart Health

ALLA KAY

Thank you for buying this e-book!

To receive special offers, bonus content, and info on new releases and other great reads sign up for our newsletters $\rightarrow$ support@how-to-cook.club

Fragrant Minestrone Soup

Beetroot Hummus

Hi!

Alla here ;)

I am very excited to bring you these recipes. They are incredibly tasty and simple, and I can't wait for you to try each one of them. As soon as you do, please let me know how you like it! I welcome all feedback, so please do not be shy. Send me an email: support@how-to-cook.club I read every email!

A healthy heart is the key to a long and full life without illness and worry, and it is as easy as giving up bad habits, moving your body more, and using products that are good for the heart.

My son has heart problems, and so I have been cooking the most delicious, healthy recipes that don't take a lot of time and only use 6 ingredients or less.

In this book, I have included the dishes that we cook regularly in our family for the prevention and support of a healthy heart.

This cookbook presents recipes that are easy to cook in a slow cooker, pressure cooker, air fryer, oven, or frying pan. You will also find daily meals for people who have heart problems or have suffered a stroke.

Medical journals and magazines make us aware of the importance of nutrients in daily meals for maintaining your heart. I took all these factors into account when creating my recipes, so **you can have a culinary book that will help you reduce cholesterol and improve heart health.**

I wish you all health and longevity!
Enjoy your meal!

With ♥, your Alla Kay ツ

Table of Contents

9

Chapter 1 «Useful and Dangerous Products for Heart Health»

When limiting fat intake, people often compensate by including other dangerous products in their diet. Some people have the misconception that some pills are enough and a strict diet doesn't need to be followed, but that is a fatal mistake. Proper nutrition is no less critical than medications. You need to be able to combine many useful products to meet the demands of the heart and blood vessels.

The first course for heart healthy eating

Carbohydrates. Few people know that foods high in carbohydrates can increase cholesterol and fat levels in the blood. Our bodies can make fat from different elements, especially carbohydrates because they are easily absorbed into the blood from the intestines. Only complex carbohydrates that aren't digested as easily are beneficial. They can be found in products made without the addition of sugar and starch and heavy processing. The best carbohydrates are found in whole grain foods. They protect the heart and blood vessels. Such grains are a powerhouse of vitamins, minerals, antioxidants, and dietary fiber.

There are two types of fiber: soluble and insoluble. Soluble fiber prevents the absorption of cholesterol in the intestines and reduces fat and sugar in the blood. Our bodies need both kinds of fibers.

Fat. The risk of cardiovascular disease is increased only by two types of fats: saturated and trans fats. Saturated, or solid, fats are natural; they are found in meat, poultry, and solid palm oil. Trans fats are practically artificial. These are seriously processed liquid vegetable oils that are made stable. They are rarely sold in their pure form, the food industry uses them widely. They are often found in margarine and finished products, hiding behind the term "hydrogenated" fats, which is always indicated in the composition on the label. Other types of fats are suitable for the heart and blood vessels, but only in moderation. In excess, they contribute to the development of obesity and are harmful to vessels.

Garnish for heart healthy eating

Cholesterol. Many cholesterol-rich foods are also rich in unhealthy fats, but hiding among them are a lot of nutrients that neutralize the harmful effects. Eggs are a prime example. It is no coincidence that today the restrictions on them have been removed, and the most stringent recommendations allow you to eat six eggs a week. Restraint in their use is necessary only for the yolks.

Vitamins. Ascorbic acid reduces inflammation in the vessels. This is especially useful for smokers and fat-lovers. Vitamin E reduces inflammation that is typical of atherosclerosis and prevents the formation of blood clots. Lack of B vitamins and folic acid increases the risk of atherosclerosis. Moreover, all reputable medical organizations emphasize that vitamins must be obtained from whole food products, and not from supplements.

Minerals. The harmful effects of sodium are well known, but many people aren't aware of which products contain a lot of it (see the figure). Potassium is an antagonist to sodium. It prevents hypertension, or high blood pressure, and strokes. Magnesium not only protects against heart disease and hypertension but also reduces blood sugar and strengthens the immune system. Calcium also has a positive effect on blood pressure, and in older women, it reduces the risk of heart attacks.

Dessert for heart healthy eating

Useful substances of plant origin. Their names are very complicated, and they hardly need to be remembered, but you can recognize the precious gifts of nature by color: such substances give a bright color to vegetables, fruits, and berries. Almost all of these substances work in similar ways. Firstly, they weaken the inflammation in the vessels. Secondly, many of them have some specific effects; they prevent the formation of blood clots, the creation of cholesterol, and the deposition of lipids. Like vitamins, it is better to get them from foods than out of pills.

Useful and harmful products for heart healthy diet

Useful:

Omega-3 fats: fatty fish (salmon, sardines, herring, trout, tuna), walnuts, flaxseed oil, rapeseed, and soy.

Monounsaturated fats: rapeseed, olive, and peanut butter.

Polyunsaturated fats: sunflower, corn, and vegetable oil.

Whole grains: bread, breakfast cereals, and other products from whole grains.

Soluble dietary fiber: legumes, rolled oats, lentils, apples, pears, and many vegetables.

Insoluble dietary fiber: bran, whole grains, the skin of vegetables and fruits.

Vitamin E: whole grains, vegetable oils, shrimp, nuts, asparagus.

Vitamin C: all citrus fruits, kiwi, strawberries, broccoli, cauliflower, bell pepper.

Folate: fruit (including citrus) and green vegetables.

Vitamin B6: Whole grains, bananas, meats, nuts, peanuts, legumes.

Vitamin B12: fish, poultry, meat, eggs, dairy products.

Carotenoids: orange, yellow, red, green fruits, and vegetables (except citrus).

Phytonutrients: vegetables, fruits, soybeans, and other legumes, whole grains, egg yolks.

Potassium: bananas, citrus fruits, vegetables, potatoes.

Magnesium: fruits and vegetables, whole grains, fish and seafood, nuts, legumes.

Calcium: dairy products and canned fish with bones

Harmful:

Saturated fats: fats in meat and other organs of meat animals, egg yolks, milk fat, chicken skin, french fries, and other fried fast food, palm and palm kernel oil, and oil of other tropical plants.

Trans fats: hydrogenated fats in many foods and margarine; many deep-fried and fast food products like donuts, pastries, pastries, crackers, and snacks on the go.

Cholesterol: liver and other organs of meat animals, yolks, fats in meat, chicken skin, milk fats (butter, cream, etc.).

Sodium: salt, soy sauce, soups (dry, in cubes, cans), ready-made seasonings for first and second courses, pickles, sausages and cheeses, fast food, snacks on the go type of chips.

Fructose: sweet foods and drinks containing high fructose corn syrup (see as part of the product).

Sugar: sugar and products with it.

Welcome to my kitchen!

Chapter 2 «Breakfast for Heart Health»

Choose one of the following:

1. Meatloaf Burgers with Tomato Sauce

Ingredients

- ½ lb. minced turkey
- 1 Tbsp. wholemeal flour
- 1 Tbsp. olive oil
- ¼ c. low-sodium chicken broth
- 1 (14.5 oz.) can diced tomatoes with garlic and onion

- ½ Tbsp. Worcestershire sauce
- 2 tsp. salt-free Montreal steak seasoning

Directions

1. Form turkey into two patties; sprinkle patties with Montreal steak seasoning.
2. Cook patties over medium heat to the desired doneness; remove from skillet and keep warm.
3. Heat oil in the same clean skillet over medium heat; add flour and cook. Stir for 2 minutes.
4. Add in the tomatoes and chicken broth and stir for 2 minutes until thickened. Stir in Worcestershire.
5. Add burgers to this sauce; cook 1 minute or until thoroughly heated.

Enjoy your meal!

Preparation: 5 min

Cook: 10 min

2. Green Beans in Oven

Ingredients

- 12 oz. green bean pods
- 1 Tbsp. canola oil and/or olive oil
- ½ tsp. onion powder
- ⅛ tsp. pepper
- ⅛ tsp. salt

Directions

1. Preheat oven to 350°F. Mix green beans with onion powder, pepper, and oil.
2. Spread the seeds on the baking sheet.

3. Bake 15 minutes or until you have a delicious aroma in the kitchen.

Enjoy your meal!

Preparation: 5 min

Cook: 15 min

3. Pistachio Fish with Crisp

Ingredients

- ¾ c. quinoa
- 4 medium pieces firm, skinless, white fish (such as tilapia or cod)
- 4 tbsp. unsweetened Greek yogurt
- ¼ c. whole-wheat panko
- ¼ c. unsalted peeled pistachios
- 2 tbsp. olive oil
- 4 c. spinach
- 2 tbsp. lemon juice
- ¾ tsp. salt and pepper

Directions

1. Preheat oven to 375°F.

2. Cook quinoa according to package instructions.

3. Meanwhile, season the fish with the mixture of salt and pepper, then brush Greek yogurt on each slice.

4. Mix whole wheat panko and shredded pistachios with olive oil. Sprinkle over fish, pressing down a little.

5. Bake on a foil-lined baking sheet for about 12-15 minutes.

6. On a separate plate, add quinoa, baby spinach, lemon juice, olive oil, and salt and pepper mixture. Mix it all up.

7. Serve the quinoa with fish.

I cook this meal every week.

Finger-licking good!

Preparation: 2-5 min

Cook: 20 min

4. Spicy Unsweetened Carrot Fritters

Ingredients

- 2 large eggs

- 12 oz. carrots, about 4 medium

- ¼ c. panko bread crumbs

- 3 scallions

- ¼ red chili, or to taste

- 1 c. cilantro

- 3 tbsp. olive oil

- ¼ tsp. mix salt and pepper

- 2 oz. feta cheese, for garnish

Directions

1. In a large bowl, beat the eggs with salt and pepper.

2. Grate carrots on a coarse grater. Combine with eggs and mix.

3. Thinly chop 2 scallions, chile, and cilantro and add to the bowl with the eggs.

4. In a separate bowl, mix the lime juice, 1 tbsp. oil, and remaining scallion.

5. Heat a cast-iron skillet over medium heat, then add 1 tbsp. oil.

6. Drop a spoonful of the carrot mixture into the skillet (the number of spoons that fits in your pan) and cook about 3 min per side until golden brown and crisp. Transfer to a paper napkin so that the remaining oil is absorbed.

7. Stir the crumbled feta onto the scallion mixture. Serve over the carrot fritters.

Looks great and tastes even better!

Mouth-watering good!

Preparation: 10 min

Cook: 6-7 min

5. Spring Vegetable Carbonara

Ingredients

- 1 ½ c. peas, frozen
- 1 lb. spaghetti
- 2 tbsp. olive oil
- ½ lb. asparagus
- 1 tsp. fresh lemon juice
- 2 large eggs
- ¾ c. grated Parmesan
- 1 tsp. freshly grated lemon zest
- 10-15 basil leaves
- ¼ tsp. mix salt and pepper

Directions

1. Boil water in a large saucepan. Add peas and cook about 2 minutes.

2. Transfer peas to a small bowl.

3. Add spaghetti to boiling water and cook 9 minutes.

4. While pasta is cooking, heat the oil in a skillet over medium heat, add pieces of asparagus, and cook, occasionally stirring, about every 3 minutes.

5. Add peas and salt, and cook 2 more minutes.

6. In a separate bowl, whisk together eggs and Parmesan. Add drained pasta and 1/2 cup water and toss to coat well.

7. Add asparagus and pea mixture, along with the lemon zest, lemon juice, and basil. Season pasta with a little pepper and additional salt, if necessary. Top with extra Parmesan and basil to taste.

Enjoy!

Preparation: 5 min

Cook: 30 min

6. Pork Medallions with Berry Sauce

Ingredients

- ½ lb. lean pork tenderloin
- ¼ tsp. paprika
- ¼ tsp. salt
- ¼ tsp. pepper
- 2 tsp. extra virgin olive oil
- ⅔ c. frozen blackberries or cowberry
- 2 tsp. balsamic vinegar
- 1 tsp. orange juice, to taste

Directions

1. Cut the pork into 1½-inch medallion slices.

2. Sprinkle pork with a mixture of paprika, salt, and pepper.

3. Cook pork in a hot skillet for 2-3 minutes per side.

4. Remove from pan, and put in a deep plate.

5. Add berries of choice, vinegar, orange juice, and remaining salt and pepper to the skillet.

6. Cook over medium heat for 5 to 6 minutes. The sauce should thicken.

7. Put a spoonful of sauce on each piece of the medallion.

Nourishing and piquant!

Bon appetit, my dear!

Preparation: 15 min
Cook: 12-15 min

7. Turkey Meatballs

Ingredients

- 1 lb. lean white meat turkey
- 1 large egg white
- ½ lemon
- 2 bell peppers, 1 red, and 1 orange
- 1 jalapeño
- 1 c. tomatoes, grape or cherry
- 1 tbsp. olive oil, preferably extra-virgin
- ½ c. Greek yogurt
- 4 thin pitas
- 4 scallions
- 2 tbsp. fresh or dry dill, fresh or dry

- 1 tsp. cumin
- ½ tsp. coriander
- ¼ tsp mix salt and pepper

Directions

1. Heat grill and line a large rimmed baking sheet with nonstick foil.
2. Mince turkey.
3. Combine the minced turkey, egg white, chopped scallions, dill, cumin, coriander, and a mixture of salt and pepper.
4. Form the mixture into 20 small meatballs and place them on the prepared baking sheet.
5. Broil 4-5 minutes.
6. Meanwhile, add in a separate bowl the peppers, jalapeño, sliced tomatoes, oil, sliced scallion, and salt and pepper. Toss to combine.
7. Spread a teaspoon of yogurt on top of each meatball. Squeeze the lemon juice over the top.
8. Sprinkle with spicy greens.

P.S. Breaking away from this dish is impossible!

Preparation: 10 min

Cook: 25-30 min

8. Tuscan Bass with Beans and Squash

Ingredients

- 4 (6 oz.) striped bass
- 12 oz. zucchini or yellow squash
- 1 c. sliced onion
- 1 can cannellini beans
- 2 garlic cloves
- 1 can tomato sauce ⅄
- ½ c. water
- 1 ½ tsp. fresh rosemary
- 1 tbsp. olive oil
- ¼ tsp. pepper

Directions

1. Heat a medium nonstick skillet.

2. Fry onions in the pan for 3 minutes. Next, add squash and fry for about 2 minutes. Add garlic and cook 1 minute until fragrant.

3. Add beans, tomato sauce, water, rosemary (crushed), and pepper; mix and bring to boil.

4. Reduce heat and place fish on top of the sauce. Cover and simmer 7-10 minutes.

5. Serve the fish on the prepared mixture.

Enjoy your meal!

Preparation: 10 min

Cook: 20-25 min

9. Mediterranean Chicken Pitas

Ingredients

- 2 ½ c. white meat chicken, cooked
- 2 piece pita bread
- 1 container hummus
- 4 medium tomatoes
- ¼ small onion
- ¾ c. parsley
- 1 tbsp. olive oil
- ⅛ tsp pepper
- ⅛ tsp salt
- For garnish:

- ½ head romaine lettuce
- ½ c. roughly chopped fresh mint leaves
- 1 large lemon

Directions

1. Before cooking, chop the boiled chicken, cut the tomatoes into 4 pieces, chop the parsley coarsely, and cut the onion into rings.
2. In a medium bowl, toss together the pieces of tomatoes, onions, oil, and salt and pepper.
3. Add the chicken and parsley, then stir to combine.
4. Split the pitas to make 4 rounds.
5. Spread each pita with hummus, then top with the lettuce and mint and squeeze the juice of half a lemon on top.
6. Gently place a spoonful of chicken mixture on top of the lettuce.

Enjoy delicious Mediterranean cuisine!

Preparation: 5 min

Cook: 10-12 min

10. Buffalo Chicken Nuggets

Ingredients

- 1 (8 oz.) boneless, skinless chicken breast
- 1 large egg white
- ¼ c. all-purpose flour
- 1 Tbsp. hot sauce
- 1 Tbsp. light butter with canola oil, melted
- ⅓ c. Greek yogurt
- 2 Tbsp. crumbled blue cheese
- 1 Tbsp. fat-free milk

Directions

1. Preheat oven to 430°F.

2. Cut chicken breast into 2-inch chunks. Lightly beat egg white.

3. Toss together chicken and egg white in a medium bowl. Add flour and mix.

4. Coat a foil-lined pan with cooking spray. Place chicken on a wire rack.

5. Coat chicken with cooking spray and bake 18 to 20 minutes or until golden brown.

6. Combine hot sauce and butter. Drizzle over chicken.

7. Mix yogurt, blue cheese, and milk.

8. Serve with chicken nuggets.

So yummy!

Preparation: 6-8 min

Cook: 18-20 min

11. Roasted Broccoli

Ingredients

- 3 c. broccoli florets
- 1 tsp. sour cream
- 2 tsp. olive oil, preferably extra virgin
- ⅛ tsp. salt
- ⅛ tsp. pepper

Directions

1. Preheat oven to 400°F.
2. Mix broccoli florets, oil, salt, and pepper in a bowl.
3. Gently place the mixture on a baking tray.

4. Bake 15 to 20 minutes or until broccoli is t

5. Serve with sour cream or Greek yogurt.

Enjoy!

Preparation: 3 min

Cook: 15-20 min

? Low fat Sour Cream

Veggie-Turkey Sloppy Joes

Ingredients

- ½ lb. turkey
- 1 carrot
- ½ c. bell pepper, chopped, green or orange
- ½ c. onion, chopped
- 2 Tbsp. tomato paste
- 2 Tbsp. water
- ½ tsp. apple cider vinegar
- 1 tsp. salt-free steak grilling seasoning
- ½ tsp. dry mustard, or use other mustard
- ⅛ tsp. salt
- 2 toasts

Directions

1. In a preheated pan, add ground turkey, carrot, bell pepper, and onion. Cook over medium heat for 5 minutes.

2. Add in tomato paste, water, vinegar, steak seasoning, mustard, and salt. Cook 5 minutes or until sauce thickens.

3. Spoon turkey mixture onto toasts.

Preparation: 5 min

Cook: 10-12 min

13. Curry Chicken Stew

Ingredients

- 1 8 oz. boneless, skinless chicken breast
- 1 Tbsp. flour
- 1 Tbsp. canola oil, or olive
- ⅓ c. coconut milk
- ½ c. bell pepper, chopped, red or orange
- 2 green onions, chopped
- ⅓ c. frozen green peas, thawed
- 1 tsp. curry powder
- ⅛ tsp. crushed red pepper
- ¼ tsp. salt
- ½ lime or lemon

Directions

1. Heat a saucepan with oil.

2. Cut chicken breast into bite-size pieces. Then add chicken in the pan and cook 3 minutes, stirring.

3. Remove chicken from pan, and set aside.

4. Mix flour and oil in a saucepan. Cook over medium heat 1 minutes, stirring.

5. Add coconut milk, chicken, bell pepper, onions, peas, curry powder, red pepper, and salt. Cook 3-4 minutes.

6. Serve with lime wedges.

Enjoy your meal!

Preparation: 5 min

Cook: 8-12 min

14. Lemon Orzo

Ingredients

- 2 oz. orzo

- 2 tsp. extra virgin olive oil

- ½ tsp. grated lemon rind

- ⅛ tsp. salt

Directions

1. Cook orzo according to package directions.

2. Toss with the oil, lemon rind, and salt

Preparation: 16 min

Cook: 5-7 hour

15. Mango Smoothie

This is the best healthy breakfast recipe you've seen. This smoothie will satiate you and provide you with enough energy for half the day.

Ingredients

- 2 medium mangoes
- 2 cups unsweetened pineapple juice
- 1 medium banana
- 3 tbsp coconut cream

Directions

1. Peel and cut the mango into slices.

2. Mix the ingredients in a blender and serve immediately.

If desired, serve with lime or mint leaves.

Bon appetit, my dear!

Preparation: 5 min

Cook: 5 min

16. Pancakes with Spinach and Carrots

Ingredients

- 3 medium potatoes
- ½ cup fresh spinach leaves
- 1 egg
- 1 small onion
- ½ carrot, peeled
- ½ tbsp cornflour
- salt, to taste

Directions

1. In a bowl, mix grated potatoes, diced spinach, onions, and carrots. Salt and mix well.

2. Squeeze the vegetable mixture to get rid of excess moisture. Add the cornflour and mix.

3. Form patties. Place the vegetable patties in a preheated pan with olive oil. Fry on both sides until cooked through and golden

Enjoy!

Preparation: 10 min

Cook: 20 min

17. Pan-Fried Potato Cakes Without Egg

Ingredients

- 3 large potatoes
- 1 tbsp cornstarch
- 1 green onion
- 2 tbsp of olive oil
- salt and ground pepper, to taste

Directions

1. Wash, peel, and chop the potatoes.

2. Fry the potatoes until golden brown in a pan with olive oil.

3. Remove the fried potatoes from the pan and mash.

4. Combine the mashed potatoes with corn starch and chopped and, chopped onion, adding salt and pepper to taste.

5. Form thick cakes and fry in a pan with the remaining oil until golden brown.

Finger-licking good!

Preparation: 5 min
Cook: 10 min

18. Easy Chicken and Broccoli Casserole

Ingredients

- 200 grams of chicken, boiled
- 15 oz bag frozen broccoli
- 200 grams nonfat sour cream
- 1 cup cheddar cheese
- 1-2 garlic cloves
- salt and pepper, to taste

Directions

1. Preheat the oven to 220 degrees Celsius.

2. Cut the chicken and grate the cheese. Dice the garlic.

3. In a bowl, combine chicken, broccoli, sour cream, cheese, and garlic. Transfer to a baking dish.

4. Bake for about 20-25 minutes.

Delicious!

Preparation: 10 min

Cook: 25 min

19. Scrambled Egg Toast

There are so many ways to have a healthy breakfast, but this is one of my favorites. It is both ultra-delicious and very satisfying.

Ingredients

- 2 slices rye bread
- ½ tbsp butter
- 2 eggs
- ⅓ cup feta cheese
- Pinch of parsley
- Pinch of dill
- ½ tbsp olive oil

Directions

1. Moisten the bread with olive oil. Place the bread rolls in a pan and simmer for 2–3 minutes, or until golden.

2. Remove the bread from the pan. Put some butter in a pan, adding eggs and chopped feta cheese. Stir frequently until the eggs are fried.

3. Spread the egg mixture atop 2 slices of bread and sprinkle with chopped herbs.

Make yourself a cup of tea and enjoy the best-fried egg toast you've ever had!

Preparation: 5 min

Cook: 5 min

20. Broccoli Fritters

Ingredients

- 1 large broccoli, in florets

- 3 eggs

- 1 cup flour

- 150 grams parmesan

- 2 garlic cloves

- salt and ground pepper, to taste

Directions

1. Salt a pot of water well and bring it to a boil. Add the broccoli and cook for 5 minutes until the florets are tender. Drain.

2. In a bowl, mix chopped broccoli, eggs, parmesan, flour, and garlic. Add salt and pepper to taste. Mix well.

3. Lubricate a heated pan with a bit of oil.

4. Spoon the broccoli mixture into the pan and give and shape to form pancakes. Fry for 1-2 minutes on each side until golden brown.

Recommended to be served with sour cream.

Smile and say cheese! ...ツ

Preparation: 5 min
Cook: 10 min

21. Tomato Salad with Crackers

Ingredients

- 5 medium, red tomatoes
- 1 cup nonfat sour cream
- 1 package saltine crackers
- Salt and ground black pepper, to taste

Directions

1. Dice tomatoes and place in a bowl. Stir in sour cream. Add pepper and salt and combine. Refrigerate until ready to serve.

2. Place crackers in a bag and roughly break.

3. Right before serving, stir in broken saltine crackers. Enjoy!

Preparation: 8 min

Cook: 5 min

22. Tomato Salad with Pomegranate

Ingredients

- 5 medium tomatoes
- 1 green bell pepper
- 2 shallots
- 2 tbsp pomegranate seeds
- 10-12 fresh mint leaves
- salt, to taste

For dressing

- 1-2 cloves of garlic
- ¼ cup olive oil

- 2 tbsp white wine vinegar
- 2 tbsp pomegranate juice
- 1 pinch of ground allspice

Directions

1. Finely chop the tomatoes and peppers. Dice and muddle shallots and mint leaves.
2. Combine tomatoes, peppers, shallots, pomegranate seeds and mint in a salad bowl. Add salt and mix.
3. Combine all the ingredients for the dressing separately.
4. Pour salad dressing into the salad bowl and mix. Serve immediately.

Preparation: 8 min

Cook: 5 min

23. Greek Salad

This heart-friendly, light salad is perfect for any time of day!

Enjoy as a light snack or even a full meal!

Ingredients

- 2 medium cucumbers
- 1 small green pepper
- ½ onion
- 3 small tomatoes
- 5 radishes
- 1 tbsp capers

- ¼ cup olive oil
- ¼ cup feta cheese
- 15-20 black Greek olives

Directions

1. Wash and chop vegetables into small pieces. Crush feta cheese.
2. Mix all ingredients in a large salad bowl. Drizzle with olive oil on top.
3. Refrigerate for approximately 40 minutes before serving.

Preparation: 5 min

Cook: 7 min

24. Avocado Salad with Tomatoes

Ingredients

- 4 ripe avocados
- 1 small red onion
- ⅓ cup fresh cilantro leaves
- 6 medium tomatoes

For the sauce:

- 1 lime or lemon
- 1 tsp apple cider vinegar
- 3 tbsp extra virgin olive oil
- sea salt and ground black pepper, to taste

Directions

1. Slice avocado and tomato.

2. Chop the onion and cilantro thoroughly.

3. In a separate bowl, mix lemon juice, apple cider vinegar, olive oil, salt and pepper.

4. Combine tomatoes, onions, and cilantro in a dish, pouring the sauce over the vegetables. Put avocado slices on top. Serve immediately.

Yum!

Preparation: 5 min
Cook: 8 min

Chapter 3 «Lunch for Heart Health»

1. Salmon in Honey-Soy dressing

Ingredients

- 2 (4 oz.) salmon fillets 4/
- ⅛ tsp. pepper   1/4
- ⅛ tsp. salt   1/4
- 1-2 tsp. honey   3T
- 1½ tsp. low-sodium soy sauce 2T
- 1 tsp. ginger, grated or pickled 1/2 T4p

Directions

1. Preheat oven to 350°F.

2. Put the foil on a baking sheet, and coat it with cooking spray.
3. Season salmon on all sides with salt and pepper. Broil 5-6 minutes until golden brown.
4. Mix honey, soy sauce, and ginger (if you use pickled, cut it finely).
5. Brush the mixture over salmon. Broil 2 to 3 minutes, or until the desired doneness.

Smells delicious!

Enjoy your meal!

Preparation: 5 min

Cook: 7-9 min

Sina Oven at 350

2. Italian Green Beans and Mushrooms on Wheat Orzo

Ingredients

- ½ c. orzo, preferably whole wheat
- ½ lb. green beans, cut into 1-inch pieces
- ½ (8 oz.) pkg sliced mushrooms
- 1 tsp olive oil ⅛ tsp salt
- ⅛ tsp pepper
- 1 garlic clove
- 1 tsp Italian aroma seasoning

Directions

1. Prepare orzo according to the instructions on the pack.

2. Roast mushrooms and beans for 5 minutes over high heat.

3. Add in chopped garlic, Italian aroma seasoning, salt, and pepper. Cook just 1 additional minute.

4. Divide orzo between 2 portions and top with a mixture of green beans and mushrooms.

It looks and tastes delicious!

Enjoy your meal!

Preparation: 5 min
Cook: 6min

3. Fragrant Minestrone Soup

Ingredients

- 2 celery stalks

- 2 leeks

- 1 onion

- 12 oz. red potatoes

- 8 sprigs thyme, fresh or dry1 lb. asparagus

- 6 oz. green peas

- 1 (15 oz.) can white beans

- ¼ tsp. mix salt and pepper

- 2 tbsp. olive oil

Directions

1. Heat Dutch oven on medium, add oil.

2. Chop celery, leeks, onion finely, and place in a Dutch oven. Add a little salt, and cook, occasionally stirring, 5-8 minutes.

3. Cut potatoes into 1/2-inch pieces. Add potatoes, thyme, remaining salt and pepper, and 6 cups water and bring to a boil. Simmer 8 minutes.

4. Add asparagus and simmer 2 minutes.

5. Add green peas and beans and simmer 3 to 4 minutes. Vegetables should be tender.

6. Remove thyme sprigs. Sprinkle soup with parsley and serve with toast (optional).

The best healthy soup in the whole world!

Enjoy your meal!

Preparation: 5-7 min

Cook: 22-25 min

4. Grill Ratatouille Salad

Ingredients

- 1 red pepper
- 1 (12 oz.) small eggplant
- 1 (6 oz.) medium zucchini
- 1 (6 oz.) small summer squash
- 1 lb. Campari tomatoes
- 2 1/2 tbsp. olive oil
- 2 tbsp. red wine vinegar
- ¼ c. fresh basil leaves, torn
- 4 c. arugula
- 2 large thick slices country bread
- 1 garlic clove

- 4 oz. white cheese, or fresh mozzarella
- ¼ tsp. mix salt and pepper

Directions

1. Heat grill to medium-high.

2. Meanwhile, slice the eggplant, zucchini, and squash into ¼-inch thick strips

3. In a large bowl, mix the vegetables with 1 ½ tablespoons oil and ½ teaspoon each salt and pepper.

4. Grill 3-4 minutes per side for the pepper, eggplant, zucchini, and squash, and 1-2 minutes for the tomatoes.

5. Transfer the eggplant and tomatoes to the bowl. Gently mix with the wine vinegar, arugula, and basil.

6. Grill the bread slices until lightly toasted, and rub the garlic clove on each slice.

7. Sprinkle on top with the mozzarella.

Sound delicious, doesn't it?

Preparation: 2-5 min
Cook: 10 min

5. Quick Kidney Bean Cheese Soup

Ingredients

- 1 (15 oz.) can kidney beans, no-salt-added
- ⅓ c. Picante sauce
- 1 tsp. ground paprika
- ½ tsp. ground cumin
- ⅔ c. water
- ⅓ c. green onions, chopped
- 2 tsp. olive oil, extra virgin
- ¼ c. shredded reduced-fat cheddar cheese

Directions

1. Combine beans, Picante sauce, paprika, cumin, and water in a medium saucepan. Bring to a boil.

2. Reduce heat; cover and simmer 5 minutes.

3. Next, remove from heat, and stir in the oil.

4. Spoon soup into serving bowls.

5. Do not forget to sprinkle with grated cheese.

Smile and say cheese! ツ

Preparation: 2-5 min

Cook: 15-20 min

. Sweet Potatoes with Salad-Brush

Ingredients

- 4 (6 to 8 oz.) sweet potatoes
- 4 radishes
- 2 medium carrots
- 1 large beet
- 1 medium Granny Smith apple
- ½ small red onion
- 2 tbsp. extra virgin olive oil1 tbsp. lemon juice
- ¼ tsp. salt and pepper, mixed
- 2 tbsp. sunflower seeds
- 2 tbsp. Greek yogurt, for serving

Directions

1. Prick each potato over with a wooden stick or knife and place it in the oven for 10-17 minutes.

2. Meanwhile, coarsely grate radishes, carrots, beet, apple, and onion.

3. Transfer the vegetables to a large bowl and toss with the oil, lemon juice, and salt and pepper mixture.

4. Place the sunflower seeds in a small skillet and cook about 2 minutes. Note: seeds must be peeled.

5. Divide potatoes into two parts. Top with the salad and then the seeds.

6. And the last detail - a spoonful of yogurt.

Enjoy your meal!

Preparation: 2-5 min

Cook: 25-28 min

7. Sweet Potato Stew with Butternut Squash

Ingredients

- 1 (12 oz.) sweet potato
- 1 onion
- 1 c. yellow split peas
- 2 large garlic cloves
- jalapeño
- 1 1 ½-in. piece fresh ginger
- ½ (about 1 3/4 lb.) butternut squash
- 1 tbsp. curry powder
- 1 tsp. ground turmeric
- ¼ tsp. salt and pepper

- ½ c. light coconut milk
- 1 c. fresh cilantro leaves
- 1 lemon

Directions

1. Peel the potato and cut into ½ inch pieces. Seed and thinly slice jalapeno. Seed, peel, and cut the squash into ½ inch pieces.
2. In a slow cooker, toss together the sweet potato, onion, split peas, garlic, jalapeno, ginger, butternut squash, curry powder, turmeric, and salt and pepper.
3. Add 4 cups water and cook, covered, until the peas are tender, about 4-7 hours.
4. Add in the coconut milk in the final twenty minutes of cooking.
5. Spoon the stew into bowls and top with cilantro and lemon wedges.

The aroma and taste are mouthwatering!

Preparation: 16 min
Cook: 5-7 hour

8. Beetroot Hummus

Ingredients

- 85g (3 oz.) chickpeas, canned in water and drained
- 1 (55g/2 oz.) beetroot, fresh
- 1 clove garlic, crushed (optional)
- 2 tsp. olive oil
- 1/2 tsp. ground cumin
- 1/2 tsp. ground coriander
- 4–5 tsp. lemon juice
- Black pepper, to taste
- Toasted wholemeal pitta bread

Directions

1. Put chickpeas, beetroot, garlic, olive oil, ground spices, lemon juice, and black pepper into a food processor.

2. Mix everything to form a thick paste.

3. Serve with toasted pita bread and vegetables.

Preparation: 5-7 min

Cook: 0 min

9. Broccoli Packets and Ginger Rice

Ingredients

- 12 oz. broccoli florets, fresh or frozen
- 2 tsp. olive oil
- ½ tsp. dried oregano
- ⅛ tsp. salt
- ⅛ tsp. pepper
- ⅓ c. brown rice, instant
- ½ tsp. ginger, grated, fresh or dried

Directions

1. Preheat broiler.

2. Put broccoli florets on a baking tray lined with foil.

3. Drizzle with oil, and sprinkle with oregano, salt, and pepper.

4. Broil 10-15 minutes. If you like broccoli only slightly crispy, cook for 7-10 minutes.

5. Meanwhile, cook rice according to package directions.

6. Mix rice with ginger.

7. Serve broccoli and rice alongside the chicken.

Preparation: 10 min

Cook: 15 min

10. Squash and Chickpea Soup

Ingredients

- 1 c. chickpeas, canned, no-salt-added
- ¾ c. red onion, chopped
- 1 (14.5 -oz.) can tomatoes with green chilies
- 2 c.ups of water
- garlic clove
- 1 Tbsp. canola oil
- 1 c. squash
- ¼ tsp. ground cumin
- ⅛ tsp. cayenne pepper
- ⅛ tsp. salt

Directions

1. Sauté onion and garlic in hot oil in a medium saucepan for 2 minutes.

2. Add squash, cumin, and cayenne pepper. Sauté 3 minutes.

3. Add chickpeas, tomatoes, and water. Cover and bring to a boil. Reduce heat to low and cook 30 minutes, stirring every 10 minutes.

4. Serve with parsley.

Enjoy your meal!

Preparation: 5 min

Cook: 35 min

11. Winter Squash and Lentil Stew

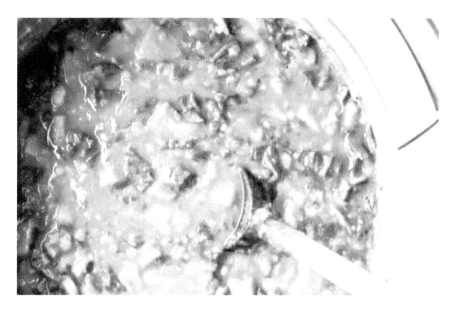

Ingredients

- 2 medium shallots
- 1 small squash
- 1 lb. green lentils, picked over
- 6 c. broth, chicken or vegetable
- 5 c. spinach
- 1 tbsp. apple cider vinegar
- 1 tbsp. ginger, fresh, finely chopped
- 1 tbsp. vegetable oil
- 1 tsp. ground coriander
- ½ tsp. ground cardamom

Directions

1. Finely chop the onion. Add shallots and ginger to a pressure-cooker pot on medium, cook in oil for 5 minutes or until shallots are golden, stirring.

2. Add coriander and cardamom. Cook for 1 minute, stirring.

3. Add squash, lentils, broth, and salt.

4. Bring the mixture to high pressure, then reduce to low. Cook 10-15 minutes.

5. Release pressure by using the quick-release function.

6. Add spinach, vinegar, and salt and pepper.

Enjoy a delicious meal!

Preparation: 5-10 min

Cook: 18-25 min

12. Hummus and Salad Pita Flats

Ingredients

- 2 (2 oz.) whole-wheat pitas
- ¼ c. sweet roasted red pepper
- hummus
- 2 eggs, hard-boiled
- 8 olives, pitted
- 1 tsp. oregano, dried
- 2 c. spring mix
- 2 tsp. olive oil, preferably extra virgin

Directions

1. Heat pitas according to package directions.

2. Finely chop the eggs and olives. Spread hummus evenly over pitas and top with eggs, olives, and oregano.

3. Toss spring mix with oil in a bowl, and transfer and arrange evenly on each pita.

Nutritious and tasty!

Preparation: 20 min

Cook: 5 min

13. Cilantro Broccoli Rice

Ingredients

- ⅓ c, brown rice, instant
- 1 c. broccoli, florets
- 2 Tbsp. cilantro, fresh, chopped
- ½ lemon
- ⅛ tsp. salt
- 1 tsp. Greek yogurt

Directions

1. Cook rice according to the package directions.
2. Bake broccoli in the oven for 6-8 minutes.

3. Toss rice and broccoli with cilantro.
4. Serve with the juice of ½ lemon and teaspoon yogurt over top.

A healthy dish can be delicious!

Preparation: 3 min

Cook: 15-18 min

14. Cilantro-Lime Avocado Salad

Ingredients

- 1 avocado

- 1 Tbsp. lime juice, fresh

- 2 tsp. extra virgin olive oil

- ⅛ tsp. salt and pepper, mixed

- 2 c. spring mix ~~lettuce~~

- 2 Tbsp. cilantro, fresh, chopped

Directions

1. Cut the avocado into slices.

2. Add spring mix and fresh cilantro.

3. Drizzle with juice of lime and oil, and sprinkle w

and pepper.

Enjoy your meal!

Preparation: 2 min

Cook: 5 min

15. Vegetable Soup

A heart-healthy diet is essential. This light vegetable soup is a perfect staple for a healthy lifestyle.

Ingredients

- 1 large, yellow onion
- 3-4 garlic cloves
- 6 medium tomatoes
- 2 medium zucchinis
- 1 yellow squash
- 2 cups corn kernels

- 6 cups vegetable stock
- ½ cup fresh basil
- juice of 1 lemon or lime
- salt and ground pepper, to taste

Directions

1. Finely chop all the vegetables.

2. In a heated saucepan, fry the onion until golden brown. Add chopped garlic and cook for about 2 minutes.

3. Add tomatoes to the pan and simmer for about 10 minutes. Add the remaining vegetables and pour in vegetable stock.

4. Bring the mixture to a boil, then lower the heat and simmer for another 15 minutes. Add basil, lemon juice, and zest.

Bon appetit, my dear!

Preparation: 10 min

Cook: 25 min

16. Light Chicken Rice Soup

Ingredients

- ½ cup rice, uncooked
- 1 small onion
- 1-2 garlic cloves
- 1 chicken, boiled and diced
- ¼ zucchini
- ½ carrot
- ½ celery stalk
- 2 tbsp olive oil
- 4-5 cups chicken stock

Directions

1. Wash and dice all the vegetables, including the garlic.

2. Pour the oil into the pan, add the onions, and simmer on low heat until transparent.

3. Add all the vegetables and rice to the pan and simmer for about 5 minutes.

4. Add chicken and salt to taste. Pour in the chicken stock, bring to a boil, then reduce the heat and let it simmer until the rice is cooked through.

This is delicious!

Preparation: 10 min
Cook: 15 min

17. Lemon Chicken Noodle Soup

Ingredients

- 2 tbsp olive oil
- 2 celery stalks
- 2 carrots
- 1-2 garlic cloves, minced
- 250 grams of chicken
- 1 package noodles
- 8 cups chicken stock
- 1 tbsp onion powder
- 4 sprigs fresh thyme
- 2 bay leaves
- 1 lemon

- ¼ cup lemon juice
- salt and black pepper, to taste

Directions

1. Dice the carrots and celery.

2. In a large preheated pan, add oil, celery, and carrots. Fry until tender, or about 7 minutes. Add garlic and onion powder, then salt and pepper to taste.

3. Add chicken stock, bay leaves, and chicken. Bring to a boil and cook until the chicken is cooked through about 15 minutes.

4. Remove the chicken and let it cool. Keep the broth on low heat.

5. Boil the noodles in the broth following the instructions on the package.

6. Shred the cooled chicken fillets and add to the pan, along with the zest and juice of a lemon.

Bon appetit, my dear!

Preparation: 15 min

Cook: 20 min

18. Cod Fish Chowder

Ingredients

- ¼ cup olive oil
- 200 grams cod
- 1 medium onion
- 1-2 garlic cloves
- 3 green onions
- 2 medium potatoes
- 3 tbsp flour
- 1 red bell pepper
- 1 yellow bell pepper
- 2 cups vegetable broth

- 2 cups of rice milk
- 1 bunch parsley

Directions

1. Peel and cut the potatoes into cubes.
2. Fry the garlic and onions in a saucepan until soft. Add chopped potatoes. Cook over low heat for 7-10 minutes. Season with salt and pepper.
3. Add in the flour while continually stirring for 6 minutes.

4. Pour in the broth and add parsley. Simmer until the soup thickens.
5. Gently add cod and cover until the fish is fully cooked.

Bon appetit, my dear!

Preparation: 12 min

Cook: 20 min

19. Leek Tomato Soup

Ingredients

- 6 large, fresh tomatoes
- 3 leeks
- 4-5 cups chicken or vegetable broth
- ¼ cup olive oil
- 1 tsp fresh basil, finely chopped
- salt and ground pepper, to taste
- 1 sprig of fresh basil, for garnish

Directions

1. Finely chop the leek and tomatoes.

2. In a saucepan, bring leeks and broth to a boil. Boil for 5-8 minutes.

3. Add tomatoes and olive oil. Lower the heat and cook for 10 minutes.

4. Serve and garnish with a sprig of basil.

Enjoy a truly unique aroma and taste!

Preparation: 5 min

Cook: 15 min

20. Crispy Chicken Salad

Ingredients

- 400 grams of broccoli
- 1 large bell pepper
- 1 large carrot
- ½ tin canned pineapple
- 2 medium fillets, boiled
- 1 cup low-fat sour cream
- ⅓ cup sunflower seed kernels
- ground black pepper, to taste

Directions

1. Chop and boil the broccoli. Dice the pepper. Grate the carrots.

2. Combine all ingredients except sour cream and sunflower seeds in a bowl.

3. Add sour cream and mix. Sprinkle sunflower seeds on top.

4. Refrigerate for 20 minutes before serving!

Preparation: 15 min

Cook: 10 min

21. Chicken Salad with Grapes

A truly delicious recipe that fits perfectly into the lifestyle of heart-healthy eating. All the ingredients are very light and tasty!

Ingredients

- 1 cup low-fat yogurt
- 2 tsp wholegrain mustard
- 2 tbsp dried apricot
- ½ tsp salt
- 400 grams of chicken, boiled
- 200 grams seedless grapes
- 50 grams almonds, toasted

- 4 celery stalks
- green onions, for garnish

Directions

1. Beat yogurt and mustard together. Add dried apricots. Stir until smooth.

2. Chop chicken fillet and almonds.

3. Put chicken, grapes, almonds and chopped celery in a serving bowl. Add yogurt dressing and mix gently. Refrigerate for 30 minutes.

4. Before serving, sprinkle with green onions.

Finger-licking!

Preparation: 10 min
Cook: 15 min

22. Baked Trout

Ingredients

- 2 medium rainbow trout fillets
- 2 tbsp olive oil
- 1 tbsp lemon or lime juice
- 1 tbsp white wine vinegar
- 1 medium onion
- 1-2 garlic cloves
- 1 pinch salt

Directions

1. Preheat the oven to 350 degrees.

2. Chop onion and garlic. Combine olive oil, lemon juice, vinegar, onion, and garlic.

3. Put the fillet in a baking dish lightly greased with olive oil, salting to taste.

4. Pour the dressing onto the trout fillets. Bake at 280 degrees for 18 minutes or until you smell a fantastic aroma from the oven. Sprinkle with dill before serving.

Enjoy!

Preparation: 10 min
Cook: 20 min

23. White Bean and Crisp Bacon Soup

Ingredients

- 3 slices bacon
- 2 c. Great Northern beans, dried
- 2 medium carrots
- ¾ c. onion, chopped
- 2 celery stalks
- 2 garlic cloves
- 3 c. low-sodium chicken broth
- ½ tsp. salt and pepper, mixed
- 1 Tbsp. rosemary, dried
- 1 bay leaf

Directions

1. Place beans in a 3-quart slow cooker.

2. In the meantime, cook bacon in a skillet over medium heat until crisp. Crumble the bacon on a separate plate.

3. Add onion, carrot, celery, and minced garlic to bacon grease in skillet; cook 3-4 minutes or until golden brown.

4. Add the mixture of onions and bacon to a slow cooker.

5. Also add broth, salt, pepper, dried rosemary, and bay leaf. Cover and cook on low for 7-10 hours or until beans are tender. Remove bay leaf, and divide into 6 servings. Cover up remaining soup and save for later.

Great meal for busy ladies!

Preparation: 10 min

Cook: 7-10 hours

24. Baked Broccoli with Parmesan

Broccoli is full of healthy vitamins for the body, and baked broccoli will retain most of the useful nutrients. Seasoned with cheese, this dish is just a blessing!

Ingredients

- 200 grams of broccoli
- 4 tbsp olive oil
- salt and ground pepper, to taste
- ¼ cup parmesan cheese

Directions

1. Preheat the oven to 220 degrees Celsius.

2. Cut broccoli into florets and mix with olive oil.

3. Season the broccoli with salt and pepper and put on a baking sheet. Bake for 20-25 minutes.

4. Remove broccoli from the oven and sprinkle with grated cheese.

Enjoy a delicious meal!

Preparation: 5 min

Cook: 25 min

Chapter 4 «Dinner for Heart Health»

1. Light Salad with Spinach and Tomatoes

This spinach and tomato salad is delicious and filled with healthy nutrients for the heart.

Ingredients

- 5-6 cups fresh spinach
- 200 grams cherry tomatoes
- ½ cup yellow onion
- 1 bunch sweet basil

- 2 garlic cloves
- 2 tsp ginger
- ½ cup olive oil
- 2 tbsp lemon or lime juice
- salt, to taste

Directions

1. Dice the onions and garlic, and put in a bowl. Add basil, ginger, olive oil, lemon juice, and salt.
2. Mix the ingredients and add the cherry tomatoes.

Bon appetit, my dear!

Preparation: 5 min

Cook: 10 min

2. Baked Greek Lemon Chicken

Ingredients

- 2 chicken breasts, bone-in, skinless
- 7 grape tomatoes
- 7 kalamata olives, pitted
- ½ c. onion, chopped
- 1 artichoke heart, frozen
- 2 tsp. olive oil
- ½ tsp. oregano, dried
- ¼ tsp. salt and pepper, mixed
- 1 lemon

Directions

1. Preheat oven to 400°F.

2. At this time, season the chicken with oregano and mixture of salt and pepper.

3. Fry the chicken in a skillet over medium heat for 2 to 3 minutes on each side, or until browned.

4. Place chicken in a baking dish coated with cooking spray. Cut the olives in half. Arrange tomatoes, olives, onion, thawed artichoke (cut into large chunks), and lemon wedges around the chicken.

5. Drizzle with olive oil. Bake 20-25 minutes or until chicken is browned. The vegetables should be tender.

A delicious Greek dish that everyone can enjoy!

Preparation: 10 min
Cook: 25-28 min

3. Leek and Lemon Spaghetti

Ingredients

- 12 oz. whole-wheat spaghetti
- 2 garlic cloves
- 2 leeks (white and light green parts)
- 1 lemon
- 1 c. frozen or fresh peas
- ¼ c. parsley, chopped
- ½ c. Parmesan, finely grated
- 2 tbsp. olive oil, preferably extra virgin
- ¼ tsp. salt and pepper, mixed

Directions

1. In a pot of boiling water, add salt. Cook the spaghetti according to package directions.

2. Meanwhile, heat the oil in a large skillet over medium heat. Add the garlic and cook 1-2 minutes.

3. Take out the garlic. Then add the leeks to the skillet and cook 6-8 minutes.

4. Meanwhile, thinly slice the lemon zest and squeeze the lemon juice into a small bowl. Set aside.

5. Add two cups of water, peas, parsley leaves, and lemon zest to skillet, and cook for 2 minutes.

6. Add the cooked pasta to a big plate. Then add parmesan, whole garlic, and pepper, tossing to combine. Top with the lemon juice.

7. Sprinkle with the parsley.

Italians have never dreamed of such pasta!

Buon appetito! ツ

Preparation: 2-5 min

Cook: 15 min

4. Spinach Salad with Tomato

Ingredients

- 4-5 c.spinach, fresh
- 6 grape tomatoes
- ¾ c. cashews, raw, unsalted
- ¼ c. yellow onion
- 2 tbsp. sweet basil
- 2 garlic cloves
- 2 tbsp. terra ginger
- 2 tbsp. lemon juice
- ¼ c. olive oil
- ¼ tbsp. sea salt (optional)
- 1 tbsp. lime juice

Directions

1. Chop the onion finely and place in a mixing bowl.

2. Chop basil, garlic, and ginger and add to the mixing bowl.

3. Add olive oil, lime juice, and salt.

4. Stir the ingredients and set bowl aside.

5. Cut tomatoes into 2 parts, and chop cashews.

6. On larger plates add grape tomatoes, cashews and gently fold in freshly washed spinach.

Yum-yum!

Preparation: 2-5 min

Cook: 5 min

5. Oven-Fried Tilapia

Ingredients

- 2 (4 oz.) tilapia fillets
- 2 Tbsp. light Ranch dressing
- ¼ c. yellow cornmeal
- 1 tsp. dill, dried
- 1 Tbsp. canola oil
- ⅛ tsp. salt

Directions

1. Wash and dry tilapia with a paper towel.
2. Preheat oven to 400 °F.
3. Combine cornmeal, oil, dill, and salt.

4. Brush both sides of fish fillets with Ranch dressing.

5. Dredge fish fillets in mixture with cornmeal, oil, dill, and salt.

6. Put the fish on a baking sheet with cooking spray and bake for 15 minutes.

Enjoy your meal!

Preparation: 15 min

Cook: 15 min

6. Marinated Vegetable Salad

Ingredients

- 3 medium tomatoes
- 1 celery stalk
- ⅓ c. red onion, diced
- 14 oz. artichoke hearts, canned
- 4 oz. roasted red peppers
- 2 Tbsp. apple cider vinegar
- 1½ tsp. oregano, dried
- 2 tsp. olive oil

Directions

1. Cut tomatoes, celery, and artichoke hearts into pieces.

2. Combine tomatoes, onions, celery, artichokes, peppers, vinegar, oregano, and oil in a bowl.

3. Cover and chill at least 30 minutes before serving.

Enjoy!

Preparation: 8 min

Cook: 30 min

7. Chunky Beef Soup

Ingredients

- 1½ lb. chuck roast, lean, boneless
- 1 (14 oz.) package frozen vegetable blend
- 1 (8 oz.) package mushrooms, sliced
- 1 (14.5 oz.) can stewed tomatoes
- ¾ c. red wine
- 1 Tbsp. balsamic vinegar
- 2 tsp. dried oregano
- ½ tsp. pepper
- 1 tsp. salt
- ⅓ c. ketchup

Directions

1. Cut meat into 4 to 6 pieces.

2. Combine meat, vegetable blend, mushrooms, tomatoes, wine, vinegar, oregano, and pepper in a slow cooker.

3. Cover and cook on low for 9-10 hours.

4. Stir in the ketchup and salt, breaking up larger pieces of meat while stirring.

5. Divide into 6 servings. Serve 2 meals and freeze remaining servings for other meals.

Good for your health!

Preparation: 10 min

Cook: 9 hour

8. Easy Broccoli and Ginger Rice

Ingredients

- 1 (12 oz.) package broccoli florets
- ⅓ c. instant brown rice
- ½ tsp. dried oregano
- ½ tsp. ginger, fresh, grated
- 2 tsp. olive oil
- ¼ tsp. salt

Directions

1. Heat the oven.

2. Spread broccoli florets on a large tray lined with a piece of foil. Drizzle with olive oil and sprinkle with oregano and salt.

3. Seal foil carefully. Bake about 15 minutes.

4. Meanwhile, cook rice according to package directions; add ginger and salt and cook 2 more minutes.

5. Serve broccoli and rice alongside the chicken.

The best-flavored rice ever!

Preparation: 10 min

Cook: 15 min

9. Carrot Salad with Bell Pepper

Ingredients

- 3 c. romaine lettuce, torn
- ⅓ c. carrot, sliced thin
- ⅓ c. bell pepper, chopped thin, red or orange
- 2 tsp. canola oil, or olive
- 2 tsp. apple cider vinegar
- 1 tsp. Dijon mustard
- 1 tsp. honey
- ⅛ tsp. salt-pepper

Directions

1. Combine lettuce, carrots, and pepper pieces in a bowl.
2. Add remaining ingredients. Drizzle dressing over salad, and mix.

Fast and incredibly tasty!

Preparation: 5 min
Cook: 0 min

10. Chicken with Red Wine, Mushrooms, and Bacon

Ingredients

- 2 bacon slices, chopped
- 1 (8 oz.) chicken breast
- 1(8 oz.) package whole mushrooms
- ⅓ c. green onions, chopped
- 1 garlic clove
- ⅓ c. dry red wine
- ¼ tsp. sugar
- ¼ tsp. thyme, dried
- 1 Tbsp. light butter with canola oil
- ¼ tsp. salt

134

- ⅛ tsp. pepper

Directions

1. In a well-heated pan, fry the bacon until crisp.

2. Remove bacon onto paper towels.

3. Cut the chicken breast into two pieces and sprinkle both sides of chicken with salt and pepper.

4. Cook in a pan with the rest of the fat after removing the bacon.

5. Cook 2 minutes on each side, then set aside on dinner plates.

6. Add mushrooms and onion to the pan and cook 4 minutes. Add crushed garlic and cook 15 seconds, stirring.

7. Stir in wine, sugar, thyme, and bacon bits.

8. Cook 2 minutes or until liquid is almost evaporated from the pan.

9. Remove from heat. Stir in salt and butter.

10. Sprinkle with remaining onions.

Bon appetit, my friends!

Preparation: 15 min
Cook: 20 min

11. Steaks with Mushrooms and Blue Cheese

Ingredients

- 1 (8 oz.) beef tenderloin steak, about 1-inch thick
- ¾ tsp. instant coffee granules 6 oz. portobello mushrooms, sliced
- ¼ c. dry red wine
- 1 tsp. Worcestershire sauce
- ⅛ tsp. salt and pepper, mixed
- ¼ tsp. sugar
- 2 Tbsp. blue cheese, crumbled
- 2 Tbsp. fresh parsley, chopped

Directions

1. Cut steak in half, crosswise.

2. Sprinkle with coffee granules, salt, and pepper.

3. Heat the pan with cooking spray.

4. Cook mushrooms 6-8 minutes.

5. Add steaks. Cook 2 minutes.

6. Reduce heat to medium. Then turn steaks, and cook another 2-3 minutes.

7. Remove from skillet.

8. Increase heat to high. Add wine, Worcestershire sauce, and sugar.

9. Cook 1-2 minutes, or until thickened. Stir in mushrooms and cook 15 seconds.

10. Spoon mushroom mixture evenly over each steak. Sprinkle with cheese and parsley.

Enjoy your meal!

Preparation: 20 min
Cook: 15 min

12. Honey-Ginger Cedar Plank Salmon

Ingredients

- 1 (2 lbs.) salmon fillet, skin-on 3 Tbsp. soy sauce, lower-sodium
- 1 lemon
- 2 Tbsp. honey
- 4 c. arugula, packed
- (4 mini cucumbers)
- 1 Tbsp. Sriracha hot sauce ~ ?
- 1 garlic clove
- 1¼ c. corn kernels, cooked
- ½ c. cilantro
- ¼ tsp. salt

138

Directions

1. Heat grill on medium.

2. Grate 1 teaspoon lemon zest and squeeze ¼ cup juice and combine zest with ginger and ½ teaspoon ground black pepper.

3. Brush mixture all over the flesh side of salmon.

4. Grill salmon for 15-20 minutes.

5. Meanwhile, in a large bowl, mix soy sauce, honey, and Sriracha.

6. To the soy mixture, add crushed garlic, lemon juice, and salt. Mix with arugula, cucumbers, corn, and cilantro.

7. Brush salmon with reserved soy mixture and garnish with arugula and lemon slices. Serve with cucumber salad.

I wish you a wonderful dinner!

Preparation: 15 min
Cook: 30 min

13. Salmon Pate on Toast

Ingredients

- 225g (8 oz.) salmon fillet, cold, poached, skinless
- 6 tbsp. low-fat soft cheese
- 1 tbsp. creamed horseradish sauce
- 1 tsp. lemon zest
- 1 tbsp. fresh parsley, chopped
- 1 tbsp. fresh chives snipped
- ⅛ tsp. ground black pepper
- Whole grain bread or toast

Directions

1. Cut boiled salmon into pieces and mash.

2. Add the low-fat soft cheese and mix together.

3. Add horseradish sauce, lemon zest, herbs, and black pepper. Mix well.

4. Serve with crusty bread or toast.

Can garnish with watercress sprigs.

Enjoy your meal!

Preparation: 8 min

Cook: 0 min

14. Red Potatoes and Sweet Spicy Cabbage Salad

Ingredients

- 10 oz. small red potatoes
- 1 Tbsp. olive oil, preferably extra virgin
- 1 garlic clove
- ⅛ tsp salt and pepper, mixed
- 1½ c. cabbage, shredded
- ⅛ tsp. red pepper, ground
- 2 Tbsp. raspberry and walnut dressing

Directions

1. Cut the potatoes into 2 parts.

2. Boil the potatoes 6-8 minutes or until tender. Potatoes can also be baked.

3. Combine potatoes, oil, crushed garlic, salt and pepper in a large bowl.

4. In a separate bowl, mix cabbage, red pepper, and dressing.

5. Serve potatoes and cabbage mixture with toast.

Enjoy your meal!

Preparation: 5 min

Cook: 8-10 min

15. Cheese and Chicken

Ingredients

- 250 grams of chicken
- 2 slices feta cheese
- 1 cup flour
- 2 eggs
- ¼ cup breadcrumbs
- 2 tbsp of olive oil
- salt and ground pepper, to taste

Directions

1. Slice the chicken. Beat the eggs.

2. Stuff the slices of cheese in the chicken fillets and season with salt and pepper. Dip the fillets in egg and then cow in breadcrumbs.

3. Put oil to the pan and heat. Add chicken and fry on both sides for about 7 minutes.

4. Place the chicken on a paper towel to absorb the excess oil. Serve.

Enjoy!

Preparation: 10 min

Cook: 10 min

16. Pan-Roasted Cod with Lemon

Ingredients

- ½ cup all-purpose flour
- 400 grams cod fillet
- 3 tbsp olive oil
- 1 cup chicken stock
- 3 tsp capers
- 1 lemon, juiced
- salt and ground pepper, to taste

Directions

1. Coat the cod fillet in flour.

2. Heat the skillet over medium heat. Grease with 2 tablespoons of olive oil and place the fillet in the pan. Fry on both sides until golden.

3. Remove the filet and place it on a plate.

4. In the empty pan, add the last tablespoon of oil, vegetable broth, parsley, capers, and lemon juice. Bring to a boil and then reduce the flame. Stew until thickened. Add the lemon zest, salt, and pepper.

5. Pour the sauce on top of the fish and serve.

Finger-licking good!

Preparation: 13 min

Cook: 15 min

147

17. Plain Olive Paste

Ingredients

- 450 grams thin spaghetti
- ½ cup olive oil
- 300 grams cherry tomatoes
- 3 green onions
- 150 grams pickled artichokes
- ¼ cups pitted olives
- ¼ cups feta cheese, chopped
- 10 fresh basil leaves
- 3-4 garlic cloves
- 1 cup chopped fresh parsley
- 1 tsp ground black pepper
- 1 pinch of salt

Directions

1. Boil spaghetti guided by the description on the package.

2. Pour the olive oil in a pan and add chopped garlic and a pinch of salt. Cook for 10 seconds while continuing to stir.

3. Add chopped parsley, halved tomatoes, and finely chopped green onions to the oil in the pan. Let cook for about 1 minute.

4. Drain the prepared pasta and add the resulting mixture with olive oil and tomatoes. Toss. Add the remaining unused ingredients and mix.

Enjoy!

Preparation: 10 min
Cook: 15 min

18. Potatoes with Parmesan

Ingredients

- 3 large potatoes
- 1 tbsp water
- 1 tbsp olive oil
- 1 medium red bell pepper
- 1 small red onion
- 1 garlic clove
- 1 small bunch parsley
- 1 small bunch rosemary
- ¼ cup parmesan cheese
- salt and ground pepper, to taste

Directions

1. Dice potatoes, peppers, and onions. Chop the garlic.

2. Put the potatoes in a microwave, add water and cover. Cook in the microwave for about 3-4 minutes until the vegetables become tender.

3. Fry onions and peppers in a pan with olive oil. Add the garlic, parsley, and rosemary. Season with salt and pepper to taste. Stir.

4. Cook while stirring frequently, until the pepper and onion soften and develop a bit of color.

5. Dry potatoes and add to the pan of vegetables. Fry until potatoes are golden and slightly crispy.

6. Remove from heat and sprinkle with grated parmesan. Cover until the cheese is melted.

Truly delicious!

Preparation: 15 min
Cook: 18 min

19. Shrimp Pasta

This is a heart-healthy recipe that is not only delicious and beautiful but also nutritious.

Ingredients

- 2 cups pasta
- 2 tbsp olive oil
- 3 green onions
- 1 small zucchini
- 2 medium tomatoes
- 500 grams of shrimp
- 12 green olives, pitted
- 1 lemon or lime, juiced

- 1 garlic clove, minced
- 1 bunch parsley

Directions

1. Boil the pasta and shrimp according to the instructions on the packages.

2. Chop onions, zucchini, and tomatoes.

3. Fry the onions in olive oil in a pan. Add the zucchini and tomatoes to the pan, and fry them for about 2-3 minutes.

4. Reduce the heat and add shrimp, lemon juice, garlic, and chopped parsley.

5. Drain the pasta, drizzle with olive oil and mix with the shrimp mixture. Top with olives and serve!

The aroma and taste are exquisite!

Preparation: 12 min

Cook: 25 min

20. Baked Trout

Ingredients

- 4 trout fillets
- ¼ cup onions, chopped coarsely
- 2 tbsp olive oil
- 1 tbsp lemon juice
- 1 tbsp white wine vinegar
- 1 tsp garlic powder
- salt, to taste

Directions

1. Preheat the oven to 350 degrees Fahrenheit.

2. Combine olive oil, lemon juice, vinegar, onions and garlic in a small bowl.

3. Place fillets in a baking dish, lightly greased with olive oil. Lightly salt the fish.

4. Pour the contents of the bowl over trout fillets.

5. Bake for 13 to 15 minutes or until fish flakes easily when tested with a fork.

6. Top off with olive oil before serving.

Enjoy!

Preparation: 10 min

Cook: 20 min

21. Light Vegetarian Pasta

This veggie pasta is a cholesterol-lowering and super-food powerhouse., Loaded with broccoli and cauliflower, this dish will leave your heart happy.

Ingredients

- 2 cups farfalle pasta
- 2 cups broccoli
- 1 cup cauliflower
- 1 medium yellow bell pepper
- ½ medium onion
- 10 cherry tomatoes
- ¼ cup feta cheese
- ½ cup extra virgin olive oil
- 1/2 lemon or lime, juiced

Directions

1. Boil pasta in 6 to 8 cups water, until tender.
2. Boil broccoli and cauliflower for about 3-4 minutes. Transfer vegetables to an ice bath and drain.
3. Chop onions and peppers.
4. In a large bowl, mix the pasta, broccoli and cauliflower, chopped bell peppers, onions, and cherry tomatoes.
5. Sprinkle with feta cheese, then drizzle a mixture of olive oil and lemon juice on top.

Finger-licking good!

Preparation: 15 min
Cook: 20 min

22. Chicken Thighs in Honey Sauce

This is the best-baked chicken recipe you have ever made. It's easy and the ingredients are always at hand

Ingredients

- 4 chicken thighs
- 2 tbsp honey
- 4-5 garlic cloves
- ⅓ tbsp olive oil
- salt and cayenne pepper, to taste

Directions

1. Preheat the oven to 180 degrees Celsius. Combine chopped garlic, honey, olive oil, salt and cayenne pepper in a bowl.

2. Marinate the chicken thighs in the resulting mixture and leave for 30 minutes.

3. Place the chicken in the oven, covered with aluminum foil.

4. Bake until cooked, about 30 minutes, then remove the foil and leave for another 15 minutes.

Bon appetit, my dear!

Preparation: 15 min

Cook: 50 min

23. Tender Lamb with Apricots

Ingredients

- 350 grams lamb, boneless, trimmed of all visible fat
- tbsp grapeseed oil
- 1 medium onion
- 1 cup vegetable stock
- tsp honey
- 1 medium eggplant
- 4 small tomatoes
- ⅔ cup dried apricots
- 1-2 garlic cloves
- tbsp fresh cilantro
- salt and ground pepper, to taste

Directions

1. Dice the lamb and onion. Grease a heated thick-bottomed skillet with butter and add the lamb and onions. Cook on low heat, constantly stirring, for 8 minutes.

2. Add chopped garlic, vegetable stock, and honey. Bring to a boil and cover. Let simmer for about 45 minutes.

3. Slice eggplant and tomatoes. Add to the pan, along with apricots. Cover and simmer until lamb is soft.

4. Slice cilantro and seasoned with salt and pepper. Serve immediately from the pan with steamed rice.

Enjoy your meal!

Preparation: 20 min

Cook: 90 min

24. Pineapple Cauliflower Fried Rice

Ingredients

- 1 medium carrot

- 1 medium red bell pepper

- 1 small sweet onion

- 3 tbsp olive oil

- 4 eggs

- 4 cups cauliflower rice

- ¾ cup frozen peas

- ¾ cup pineapple

- 1-2 garlic cloves

- ½ tbsp soy sauce, gluten-free
- 1 tsp sesame oil
- 2 tbsp rice wine vinegar

Directions

1. Chop carrots, peppers, onions, and garlic.

2. Add 2 tablespoons of olive oil to a heated pan, along with onion, carrots and bell pepper. Fry everything over medium heat until vegetables are tender.

3. Add garlic and fry for another 1 minute.

4. Beat the eggs.

5. Move the vegetables aside and add another tablespoon of olive oil to the pan. Pour in the eggs and cook.

6. In a medium bowl, mix soy sauce, sesame oil, and rice wine vinegar.

7. Add the resulting sauce and cauliflower rice to the pan. Cook until rice becomes slightly crunchy, 7-8 minutes.

8. In the last minutes of cooking, add frozen peas and slices of pineapple.

Serve the rice with green onions or cilantro and enjoy!

Preparation: 10 min

Cook: 20 min

CHAPTER 5 «Sides or Small Meals for Heart Health»

1.Tomatoes Stuffed with Cream Cheese and Tuna

Ingredients

- 3 tomatoes
- 150 grams low-fat cottage cheese
- 1 can of tuna
- 2 green onions
- 1 tsp grape vinegar
- 1 tbsp olive oil
- 1 large orange
- salt and ground pepper, to taste

Directions

1. Cut the tomatoes lengthwise and remove the pulp.

2. Mash the cottage cheese with tuna and season with green onions, salt, and pepper.

3. Stuff the resulting mixture into tomatoes and drizzle with vinegar and olive oil.

4. Serve with slices of orange.

Enjoy your meal!

Preparation: 5 min

Cook: 5 min

2. Herb Roasted Zucchini and Carrots

Ingredients

- 2 medium zucchini
- 1 yellow pumpkin (squash?)
- 2 carrots
- 1 tbsp fresh oregano
- 2 tbsp fresh thyme leaves
- 2 tbsp olive oil
- salt and ground pepper, to taste

Directions

1. Preheat oven to 180 degrees Celsius.

2. Chop all the vegetables and add to a bowl, mixing with olive oil, salt, pepper, and herbs.

3. Spread the vegetables on a baking sheet and bake for about 25 minutes until they are a little brown and crispy.

Serve and enjoy!

Preparation: 10 min

Cook: 25 min

3. Baked Avocado

This simple healthy recipe will not leave anyone hungry. It is delicious and still light!

Ingredients

- 1 avocado, ripe
- 10 cherry tomatoes
- 2 slices fresh mozzarella
- 2-4 tbsp fresh basil
- 3 tbsp olive oil
- 2 tbsp balsamic vinegar
- salt and ground pepper, to taste

Directions

1. Half the avocado and remove the seed. Dice the tomatoes.

2. Put the avocado in a preheated oven to 200 degrees Celsius.

3. Put half of the chopped tomato in the avocado halves. Sprinkle with vinegar.

4. Sprinkle with fresh basil and lay the cheese slices on top.

5. Put the remaining tomatoes on top of the cheese. Drizzle with vinegar and olive oil. Finish with basil.

6. Bake for 15 minutes. Allow to cool and then serve.

Enjoy!

Preparation: 10 min
Cook: 15 min

4. Egg Salad

Ingredients

- 4 large eggs, hard-boiled
- ½ chicken, boiled
- ¼ cup nonfat sour cream
- 1 tsp Dijon mustard
- 1-2 garlic cloves
- 2 green onions
- 1 pinch of sea salt
- black pepper, to taste
- 6 lettuce leaves

Directions

1. Dice the eggs and place them in a bowl. Add sour cream and Dijon mustard, minced garlic, diced green onions, salt and pepper to a bowl.

2. Mix everything well.

3. Scoop the mixture onto lettuce leaves. Sprinkle chopped chicken on top.

This is absolutely delicious!

Preparation: 10 min

Cook: 5 min

5. Sandwich with Tomatoes

One of the simplest healthy recipes in my book.
In just 5 minutes, a great breakfast is ready!

Ingredients

- 4 slices rye bread
- 1 pinch ground black pepper
- 1 medium tomato
- ½ avocado
- 8 slices cheese of choice

Directions

1. Cut the avocado and tomato into slices.

2. Put a slice of cheese on the bread, then a layer of avocado, another layer of cheese, and a layer of tomato. Sprinkle with pepper and add the top slice of bread.

3. Put the bread in a dry pan and fry for about 3-4 minutes, or until the dough becomes slightly crispy.

Delicious!

Preparation: 5 min

Cook: 5 min

6. Zucchini and Lemon Pizza

Simple and healthy recipes are, as always, the most delicious. This effortless to prepare and insanely delightful pizza will appeal to everyone.

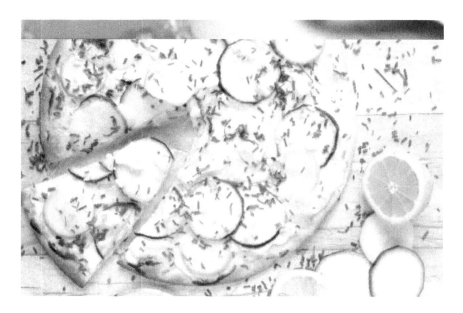

Ingredients

- 1 ready-made pizza base
- 3 tbsp Greek yogurt
- 40 grams cheddar
- 2 tbsp lemon or lime juice
- ½ green zucchini
- ½ yellow zucchini
- 30 grams of soft cheese

- ½ lemon
- 3 tbsp fresh chives
- salt and ground pepper, to taste

Directions

1. Preheat the oven to 200 degrees Celsius. Roll out the base for the pizza onto a tray.

2. Combine Greek yogurt, half of the grated cheddar cheese, lemon juice, salt, and pepper. Spread the mixture onto the base.

3. Slice the zucchini and place it on top of the mixture. Layer the remaining cheddar and soft cheese on top.

4. Sprinkle with chopped green onions and bake for 10-13 minutes.

5. Garnish with more onions and lemon zest before serving. Enjoy!

Preparation: 10 min

Cook: 15 min

7. Radish Salad

Ingredients

- 1 large radish
- 1 large cucumber
- 1 lb. sugar snap peas
- 1 lemon or lime, juiced
- ⅓ tbsp olive oil
- 1-2 garlic cloves, minced
- 2 tbsp spinach

Directions

1. Wash and cut the radish and cucumber into thin slices. Cut the peas in half.

2. In a large bowl, toss together radishes, cucumbers and peas.

3. In a small bowl combine lemon juice, oil, minced garlic, and spinach.

4. Add lemon juice mixture to salad. Refrigerate for at least 1 hour before serving.

Yummy!

Preparation: 5 min

Cook: 10 min

8. Tuna in a Tortilla

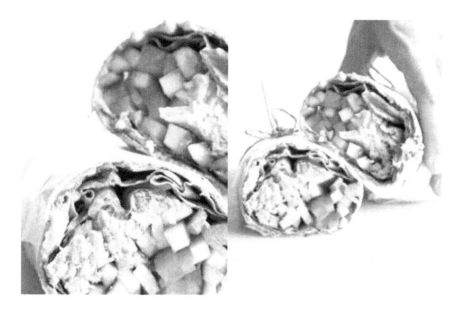

Ingredients

- 2 large whole wheat tortillas
- ½ avocado
- 100 grams of boiled tuna, boiled or canned
- 50 grams nonfat sour cream
- 6 lettuce leaves
- 1 medium cucumber
- 1 medium bell pepper
- ½ bunch cilantro
- ½ tbsp olive oil
- sea salt, to taste
- cumin, to taste
- ½ lime or lemon

Directions

1. Chop the avocado and mix with sour cream.

2. Thinly slice the pepper and cucumber. Wash and dry lettuce.

3. Lay a cling film down and place on a layer half the tortillas.

4. Put lettuce, cucumber, tuna and bell peppers on top of the tortillas. Add the avocado mixture. Salt to taste and season with spices and herbs.

5. Roll the wrap together using the cling film.

Cut in half and you can enjoy!

Preparation: 10 min

Cook: 10 min

9. Green Beans with Pine Nuts

Green beans are very good for the heart and serve as a great staple food in a healthy lifestyle

Ingredients

- 500 grams green beans, frozen or fresh
- 2 tsp olive oil
- 1 green onion
- 1-2 garlic cloves
- 3 tbsp pine nuts
- 1 tbsp red wine vinegar

Directions

1. Chop the onion and garlic.

2. Wash fresh beans and trim ends. Steam the beans for about 6-8 minutes. For frozen green beans, follow package instructions for cooking.

3. Heat oil in a skillet. Add green onions, pine nuts, and garlic. Sauté everything until golden brown.

4. Remove from heat and add vinegar. Put the beans on a dish and add a spoonful of onion mixture.

Enjoy your meal!

Preparation: 6 min

Cook: 10 min

10. Broccoli with Pine Nuts

This is one of the most straightforward and healthy recipes. It is easy to prepare and does not require a substantial investment of time.

Ingredients

- 1 broccoli head, in florets
- 2 tsp olive oil
- 1 green onion
- 1-2 garlic cloves
- 3 tbsp pine nuts
- 3 tbsp raisins
- 1 tbsp red wine vinegar

Directions

1. Trim the ends and peel the stems of the broccoli. Place in a saucepan and cook for about 5-7 minutes.

2. Chop green onions and garlic.

3. Place onions, garlic, raisins and pine nuts in a heated pan with olive oil. Simmer over medium heat until nuts turn golden.

4. Remove from heat and add wine vinegar. Spread broccoli on top and mix.

Enjoy!

Preparation: 7 min
Cook: 12 min

CHAPTER 6 «Snacks for Heart Health»

Plan Your Meals.

I love snacking, and I can chew all day long. However, in any meal, it is essential to maintain a balance of carbohydrates, fats, and proteins. As I travel a lot, I have learned to take food with me, so that when I go hungry, I will not be tempted by the siren call of a chocolate bar.

I like dried fruits and vegetables, but not dried fruits from supermarkets, which are full of preservatives. In California, there is a company that dries fruits and vegetables without additives: peaches (I love them), strawberries (second on my list of preferences), mangoes, apples, cherries (great taste!), blueberries (delicious), and persimmon. They also produce sweet and crunchy snack bars from carrots, corn, fresh pepper, and tomatoes. They taste like unusual, but yummy popcorn. I always keep a stock in the drawer and my bag. If you eat some dried vegetables or fruits (carbohydrates), some low-fat cheese, and a couple of nuts, you get a well-balanced snack.

Here are some more recipes for healthy heart snacks:

Eggs stuffed with hummus (chickpea paste): cut the eggs, remove the yolk, put 1 Tbsp. hummus inside. Add paprika to taste.

Low-fat cottage cheese paired with almonds or macadamia nuts.

Low-fat yogurt and nuts.

Ham and apple roll with macadamia or three almond nuts.

30g of Chechil cheese and half a cup of grapes.

Squirrels

- 1/4 cup low-fat cottage cheese
- 1 ounce partially fat-free mozzarella
- 2 ½ ounces of ricotta low-fat cheese
- 1 ounce chopped meat (turkey, ham)
- 1-ounce tuna canned in water
- 1-ounce low-fat soft cheese

Carbohydrates

- ½ apple
- 3 apricots
- 1 kiwi
- 1 tangerine

- 1/3 cup fruit cocktail
- ½ pear
- 1 cup strawberries
- ¾ cup blueberries
- ½ orange
- ½ cup grapes
- 8 cherries
- ½ nectarine
- 1 peach
- 1 drain
- ½ cup chopped pineapple
- 1 cup raspberry
- ½ cup blueberries
- ½ grapefruit
- 1-2 crackers without fat

Fat

- 3 olives
- 1 macadamia nut
- 1 tbsp. guacamole
- 3 almond nuts
- 6 peanuts
- 2 halves of pecans
- 1 tbsp. peanut butter

Afterword

Huge thank you 1000 times over to all the people who worked for this book to be published: designer, proofreader, photographer, my family, my friends. And to my 625,000+ funs, the devoted WomenBeautyClub subscribers - THANK YOU! THANK YOU! THANK YOU!

YOUR SUPPORT IS VERY VALUABLE AND APPRECIATED!

I tried to collect the best recipes to diversify your diet. I look forward to hearing when you recreate my recipes. And also I am waiting for your wishes and feedback with photos of cooked dishes.

Please leave a review about my book at Amazon.

✉ If you want to receive (absolutely free) new recipes from me every week, **subscribe to the tasty newsletter** → support@how-to-cook.com   I will try to surprise you! ツ

See you soon, my new friend!

Made in the USA
Middletown, DE
28 September 2021